A
DORSET DOWNS
WALK

ALAN PROCTOR

Drawings by
Dennis Brierley

First published by

THORNHILL PRESS
Cheltenham
in 1982

ISBN 0 904110 96 6

Printed by
Logos Ltd.
Cinderford

ACKNOWLEDGEMENTS

My thanks to all who helped me, on the way and in other ways: My 'support crew' for collecting me by car on a Bank Holiday, and my wife for putting up with me, and my absence.

A.P.

FOLLOW THE COUNTRY CODE

JOIN THE RAMBLERS ASSOCIATION

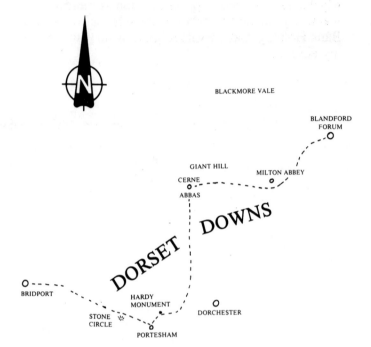

BLACKMORE VALE

BLANDFORD
FORUM

GIANT HILL

CERNE   MILTON ABBEY

ABBAS

DORSET DOWNS

BRIDPORT

HARDY
MONUMENT

DORCHESTER

STONE
CIRCLE

PORTESHAM

Descriptive text is on pages 6 to 18
Maps for the whole route are on pages   to
The total distance of this walk is about 47 miles.
NORTH is always at the top of the map.

INTRODUCTION

There is only a short introduction to this book. I let the first quote "Dorset grows on you" say it. Just let me say that the 47 miles from Blandford Forum to Bridport, alone over a long weekend, was one of the most enjoyable walks I have ever been on. "In quite a mystical way" I enjoyed the quiet, the views, the solitude, the hills and the valleys. The swift laughing little rivers, and for most of the walk easily-opened gates and good stiles. Dorset County Council are to be congratulated. In the words of somebody famous "I shall return". Again and again I hope. I don't remember seeing so many wild flowers. I have a happy memory of standing in the Dorsetshire Gap watching a deer watching me. Perhaps I was in an ebullient mood that weekend, but people seemed friendlier and kinder or perhaps it was "a mystical way".

A.P.

DORSET GROWS ON YOU

"Traverse the hills and valleys, not by car, but on foot...explore the towns and villages... Dorset grows on you in quite a mystical way."

Norman Wymer
(A Breath of Dorset, 1948)

"It is a county of dairies. Everywhere are there cows, for the smell of cows is the incense of North Dorset."

Frederick Treves
(Highways and By-ways in Dorset, 1920)

"Lobster and Dorset cream are not the right food for pilgrims. I believe the crusades could have been stopped by a Dorsetshire tea."

H.V. Morton
(In Search of England)

Blandford Forum

The town lies to the south of Cranborne Chase, and at the eastern end of the North Dorset Downs. Both the A354 Salisbury - Dorchester, and the A350 Poole - Shaftesbury roads pass through the town. Its Georgian appearance is mainly due to fire which in the eighteenth century destroyed the old town.

Blandford is a good town to wander around. There is 'The Old House' built in 1661 for the German born Dr. Sagittary.

BRYANSTON SCHOOL

Up the hill on the way to Salisbury are the Ryves Almshouses, built in 1682. Alfred Stevens the sculptor was born in the town. At the end of the Market Place near the sixteenth century church of St. Peter and St.Paul stands a monument, also by the churche's builder, John Bastard's pump and fire monument has an inscription part of which reads "raised this town like a Phoenix from its ashes, to its present beautiful and flourishing state." The Dorset Book Shop in the Market Place can sell you a guide to the town, quite apart from being an Aladdin's cave.

Lace was made in the town until 1811; Blandford bone lace was considered by Defoe to be as fine as any he had seen. Button making was a Dorset cottage industry, and Blandford was no exception. At one time there were four button makers in the Market Place. In 1770 the inhabitants of Blandford workhouse, three men and eleven women, made fifteen gross of large and small buttons in the month of June.

In 1848-9 the Lunacy Commissioners visited the town, among many other places I hasten to add; six lunatics were held. Cerne Abbas had three.

FIRE MONUMENT

That Merry Monarch Charles held a series of reviews all over Dorset. The 700 strong 1st Battalion Dorset Volunteers assembled at Blandford Forum for military exercises. During the agricultural riots in 1830 a troop of Lancers was based here. In 1831 the Dorset Yeomanry were re-enrolled to cope with riots and unruly behaviour of labourers in pursuit of higher wages.

LOWER BRYANSTON FARM

At the very western edge of the town lie green meadows on the banks of the River Stour. On the opposite bank, is a steep wooded slope named 'The Cliff'. At the northern end of this magnificent stand of trees is Bryanston School. Built for the Viscount Portman in 1890, it became a school in 1927. The fortunes of the Portman family changed, according to superstition, when they caused the old house to be pulled down to build the new one, now the school. In doing so they disturbed the ghost of 'Aunt Charlotte'. It has also been reported that sometimes the lodge gates would open and a phantom coach would go up the drive. Another fanciful tale is that if the peacocks left Bryanston the Portmans would soon follow, like the British and the Gibraltar apes.

Soon after the peacocks were sold the third Viscount died. The family sold the house and part of the estate.

Accommodation: Lower Bryanston Farm B & B near the start of the walk. The Crown Hotel, 1 West Street, an A.A. listed four star hotel.

Early closing day: Wednesday. Market day: Thursday.

NEAR QUARLESTON DOWN

7

Winterborne Stickland

We cross the River Winterborne about a half mile south of the village centre, the second village along the course of the river which has no less than nine hamlets or villages which take its name. The Winterborne joins the River Stour at Sturminster Marshall.

Winterborne Stickland has an unmistakable centre with lime trees and the base of an old cross. The church was begun in the thirteenth century. In the vestry is a large tomb with a black marble top, a memorial to Thomas Skinner who died in 1756. He lived at Quarleston Farm, we pass close by, which dates back to the thirteenth century.

QUARLESTON FARM

The village has modern houses and bungalows on the outskirts which give one the impression of the approach to a small town. Just about a quarter of a mile off route, on the southern edge of the village, is the Crown Inn, and also a food store. There was once a Winterborne Quarel, no doubt taking its name, as did the manor, from the Quarel family, which existed in 1232 A.D.

Milton Abbas

ST. CATHERINES CHAPEL

We approach via Milton Park Wood and pass the Milton Manor Hotel, A.A., R.A.C., and R.A., two stars. Near the top of Village Street is Wyvern House offering Bed and Breakfast and the Hambro Arms Public House.

The village was built by Lord Dorchester in 1771. Not just another village that was moved at the whim of its owner. It took that gentleman twenty years to acquire the houses of the old village as the houses fell vacant. It took some litigation as well; one owner accused his Lordship of flooding him out. A new church was built for the villagers using stone from the old tithe barn. This was possibly one of the very first attempts at building a model village. It is very pleasant and caters for tourists by way of a gift shop, art exhibition and rural life museum which do not intrude.

MILTON ABBEY

Copies of "Illustrated Guide to Milton Abbas' are on sale.

Not to be missed if you can possibly spare the time is Milton Abbey. It stands just over a half mile off route to the north west, and was the original site of the village. Near the Abbey church is a map of the old village.

Milton Abbey was founded in 932 by King Athelstan as a college of canons; it later became a Benedictine Monastery. A school, which had about seventy pupils, was closed towards the end of the eighteenth century following objections from the Earl of Dorchester. The school was too close to his house. Among his objections he included an assault on the character of the school's headmaster. It was alleged that the headmaster had allowed the school building to deteriorate to the point at which it was unsafe for the pupils. The poor headmaster had evidently used his floorboards and doors as fuel. His Grace also complained that the boys climbed over his walls to steal fruit and eggs. Thomas Masterman . Hardy, Admiral Nelson's Flag Captain, was one of the supposed ring-leaders. The main building is a school now; no doubt, the pupils are better behaved, and the building in better repair. This was the location site for the T.V. series 'To Serve Them All My Days'.

ALMSHOUSES MILTON ABBAS

Saint Catherine's Chapel stands in the woods above the

9

MILTON ABBAS CHURCH

church. A flight of grass steps lead up to it and from the chapel one gets a splendid view of Milton Abbey church. St. Catherine's was originally a Saxon chapel, its varied career includes rebuilding by the Normans and a spell as a labourer's cottage before it became a workshop and finally a store. It has been repaired and restored.

King George III visited Milton Abbas during his travels about Dorset to the various military reviews, which came about when the militia and cavalry were held in readiness to counter the threat of invasion from France.

Melcombe

Three hamlets, Bingham's Melcombe, Melcome Bingham, and Higher Melcombe. The church is at the first one, Bingham's Melcombe, and becomes visible as we drop down the side of Coombe Hill. Coombe Hill was once one of the beacon hills. Melcombe Bingham is next and we emerge onto the winding lane near the hamlet centre. Close by is a Post Office Stores and Vine Cottage, which has a B & B sign. North East, towards Anstey Cross, is the Fox Inn, R.A. listed, which offers accommodation, food and bed and breakfast, three quarters of a mile off route. Higher Melcombe has an old manor house and stands close by one of the oldest tracks in Dorset. A half mile on is the Dorsetshire Gap, a deep cut through the surrounding hills.

MILTON PARK WOOD.

This is a very rewarding area to take one's time and tread softly.

An abundance of wild flowers grace the banks and in the still, early mornings and evenings plenty of birds and wildlife, large and small, to enjoy.

Cerne Abbas

The village lies quietly just off the A352 Dorchester - Sherborne road. Ethelmaer, Earl of Cornwall, founded the original abbey in AD987. Of course the usual growth went with the abbey, and what must have amounted to a small town grew round it, holding an important place in the lives of the surrounding community.

CERNE ABBAS CHURCH

Quite apart from the fourteen pubs, there was a magistrates' court, a malt house and a grain market. There was a tannery, and following from that, the making of gloves, harness and boots. Queen Victoria had a pair of button boots made here.

The last stagecoach passed through Cerne Abbas in 1855 and the railways never came; they used the next valley. The township and its population declined. Now it is a neat and tidy tourist attraction "without being vulgar about it". Perhaps the virility of the Giant prevents the entire decline. The Giant has caused comment, speculation and, no doubt, shock, among many people. He is ancient, but whether Roman or older is unsure. Folklore has him as a fertility symbol so this could possibly make him older than he would be if the other suggestion is true, that he is a Roman God, Hercules, dating from AD191. Yet another authority suggests that the Romans merely added the club. A prominent figure, a titled landowning safari-park operator from Wiltshire, is reputedly proud of siring a daughter thanks to the aid of the Giant.

PATHWAY TO GIANT HILL

11

CERNE ABBAS

Folklore decrees that women wanting to be sure of bearing children should sit, or sleep, on the Giant's appropriate appendage.

Legend tells of a secret passage from the Abbey up to Cat and Chapel Hill. Cat and Chapel may be a corruption of St. Catherine's Chapel, so perhaps the passage went between Abbey and Chapel.

Another old superstition among Dorset folk was that it was beneficial to plunge a new born infant into a cold spring, due care being taken that other things were in accord. There is one such in the parish of Cerne Abbas, facing east, that fulfilled the requirements. The newborn infant could be plunged just as the rays of the rising sun touched the water.

When local shepherds bemoaned the fact that Cerne Abbas provided neither water nor beer St. Augustine asked what they would like. When the shepherds replied "water" St. Augustine struck the ground with his staff. Upon that instant a clear spring arose. Since that time St. Augustine's well has provided some of the purest water in the area. Bed and Breakfast at Giant's Head Farm, R.A. listed. There are two hotels offering meals and B & B.

Nether Cerne

South of Cerne Abbas by one and a quarter miles. A tiny hamlet of a few cottages, manor house and church. Its late thirteenth century flint church of All Saints has a Norman font, it is now cared for by the Redundant Churches Fund. The manor house, circa. 17th century, stands beside the church on a nice grassy area.

NETHER CERNE CHURCH & MANOR

In 1642 a thief stole seventy sheep from the common fields of the parish. It is an extraordinary fact that while sheep stealing was a felony and could carry the death penalty, pig stealing was only considered petty larceny.

Godmanstone

BRADFORD PEVERELL VILLAGE HALL

Less than a mile further south is the hamlet of Godmanstone. Its claim to fame is the smallest pub in England. The story is that The Merry Monarch, Charles II, stopped by a smithy and asked for a drink. The blacksmith had to refuse as he had no licence. Charles granted him a licence on the spot. The Smith's Arms had been created.

Bradford Peverell

Lies just off the A37 road, just over two miles west of Dorchester. A Roman aqueduct ran through Bradford Peverell on its way to Dorchester. The Dorset historian John Hutchins, M.A., was born here in 1698. He wrote 'A History of Dorset' in four volumes; in the index names of people alone amount to no less than eight thousand. The village lies on the banks of the River Frome which empties into Poole Harbour.

BRADFORD PEVERELL CHURCH

MARTINSTOWN CHURCH
IN RETROSPECT

Martinstown

Or Winterborne St. Martin. Here we cross another River Winterborne, the South Winterborne in this case. There seem to be about six villages taking the name. A winterborne meant that the water was usually borne in winter.* The church has a twelfth century font.

* i.e. the water flows in winter but dries up in summer.

13

Hardy Monument

HARDY MONUMENT.

Not to the novelist, but to Admiral Thomas Masterman Hardy, old boy of Milton Abbas School, Lord Nelson's Flag Captain. It was this Hardy in whose arms Lord Nelson died. The monument is a seventy feet tall octagonal stone tower erected in 1844. It has been likened to a factory chimney by more than one pundit. Seven hundred feet, or two hundred and thirty seven metres if you prefer, up on Black Down it can be seen by passing sea-farers, a fact that would, no doubt, have pleased the Admiral. He was born in Kingston Russell House between Long and Little Bredy three miles north west.

Black Down was the site of a beacon, one of a chain set up in 1804 to spread the alarm should the French invade. It was once possible to climb to the top of the Hardy Monument, the steps are now closed, but good views may be had from the top of the down and on the way down. Weymouth, Chesil Beach, Portland and Abbotsbury can all be seen. On the way down to Portesham, we shall pass by the Hell Stone, a wrongly re-erected dolmen, probably over 5,000 years old. It may have been dedicated to Hel, the goddess of the dead.

Portesham (or should it be Portisham?)

Admiral Hardy lived here as a boy, and again later in his life. His home was the 17th century manor house to the west of the church. He called the village his 'beloved Possum', this is possibly a corruption of the local dialect. Portesham has an increasing number of modern houses and bungalows, but many old cottages

THE HALF MOON, PORTESHAM

PORTESHAM.

of mellow grey stone, and a dismantled and forlorn railway bridge. There is a delightful pool set in a green at the top of the village, too grand to be a mere duck pond. Obviously well cared for, it has a box in the middle set with plants and designed to be a secure nesting place for the ducks or moorhens. A stream gurgles and chuckles down a long-side the road leading past the fifteenth century church. A delightful village for an evening stroll round. The Half Moon Inn near the church, and further down the King's Arms offer food. I had a good meal at the King's Arms. There are quite a few Bed and Breakfast houses in the village; R.A. listed is Mrs Beale at Lawtie-Springhead, at the top of the village near the pool. I stayed at Mrs Cobb's in Winter Lane and was very comfortable. There is a Post Office and shop at the top end by the pool.

Tenants Hill

As we climb up out of Portesham to cross a minor road off route, a half mile north east is the Valley of Stones. There is a great mass of sarsen stones strung out along the valley floor. The whole area is a mass of megaliths, barrows, earthworks and tumuli, though the

STONE CIRCLE

only ones we shall see on this stretch are the Stone Circle on Tenants Hill, signposted as 'Kingston Russel Stone Circle' and the remains of the enclosure close by.

Down in the valley, to our right but hidden by a hill, is Little Bredy the birthplace of the River Bride. Bridehead Park taps the infant river to make Bridehead Lake before the river pursues its hasty eight mile course to the sea at Burton Freshwater via Burton Bradstock. I was informed that the owner of the park permits public access to view the lake and springs. A good view of Kingston Russell House is obtained from the walk before a diversion up the coombe to Long Bredy. Both Long and Little Bredy take their names from the river.

Pins Knoll

Just past the White Horse Hotel and Youth Hostel near Litton Cheyney is Pins Knoll. Unfortunately, although it is only just off route we get no sign of it. There was a small iron age farm and some first century A.D. burials. The site was excavated in 1959 and evidence found also of a Romano-British building dated at fourth century A.D. Leaving Pins Knoll we drop to a valley and up the other side is **Chilcombe.** The farm and cottages are visible ahead, but not the church. A Tudor manor house was lost to us in 1939 when it was pulled down. All that remain now are the farm and the two cottages. Chilcombe church is interesting, it is one of the smallest in England. It has a fourteenth century Norman font, and there are memorials in the church to two local families – the Bishops and the Strongs. One Bishop was M.P. for Bridport in the reign of Charles II. About a quarter of a mile north is Chilcombe Hill with its unexcavated hill fort.

Shipton Gorge

The church can be seen from a distance on the approach to the village; it stands high on a mound. It probably deserves a better deal - it must be bypassed by many as Bridport is only two and a half miles away. I passed through on a Sunday afternoon and all was quiet so I did not stop. There is a Post Office Stores, some Bed and Breakfast signs and the New Inn which does accommodation and bar food according to its sign. You could try Mrs Owen, West Court, Shipton Gorge, for Bed and Breakfast and Evening Meal.

SHIPTON GORGE

BRIDPORT TOWN HALL.

Bridport (Port Bredy)

"Bridport has no history"-
Black's Guide to Dorsetshire.

Market Day Wednesday, early
closing Thursday.

The town was once a busy port,
there is now only a tiny harbour at
West Bay. There are some interesting old buildings dating back
century by century to the fifteenth.

Bridport has had an eventful past, and a visit to Bridport Museum
and Art Gallery in South Street will be worthwhile. Here the past of the
town is well documented and the exhibits reflect the local history. Part
of the Art Gallery comprises a doll collection, with dolls from all over
the world.

One of the age-old cottage industries of the area was net
making, and Bridport was the administrative centre. Ropes have
been made in the town since the thirteenth century, and the Bridport
Dagger was the grisly name given to a rope used by the hangman.
Following the Bloody Assize nine men were taken to Bridport to be
hanged.

In 1588 a small force of militia was maintained in the town. In 1668
one Robert Knight, a collector of the hearth tax, was murdered at
Bridport. As the tax collectors entered the town a crowd of men, women
and children followed them throwing stones. The unfortunate Robert
Knight was struck twice on the head and died.

In 1685 there were skirmishes in and around the town during
Monmouth's rebellion, and the town was at different times used by
both sides.

Charles II narrowly escaped capture by the Roundheads at the

George Inn, where he had been staying. A stone commemorating his flight stands at the corner of Lee Lane and the Dorchester Road.

There is a Youth Hostel in town and a camp site at West Bay. The R.A. recommend Eleven St. Andrews Road, (Mrs. H. Taylor), and the Britmead House Hotel. The latter is also listed by A.A. and R.A.C.

THE MAPS

The maps in the guide are drawn, as almost all maps are drawn, with the north at the top of the page. It is very inconsiderate of any of us to walk south, it means the map is upside down. Many people consider that it is best to draw guides so that the book can always be held in front of you the right way up. That means that on any given page north could be in any direction on the map. But what happens if the section has a sharp turn in it? Does the walker have to walk sideways? Confusing, isn't it? I repeat, the maps in this guide are drawn conventionally with north at the top of the page.

SYMBOLS ON THE MAP

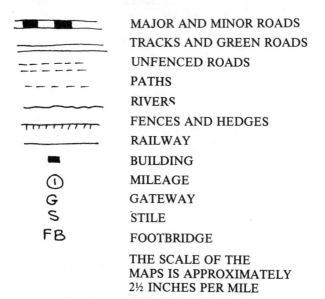

	MAJOR AND MINOR ROADS
	TRACKS AND GREEN ROADS
	UNFENCED ROADS
	PATHS
	RIVERS
	FENCES AND HEDGES
	RAILWAY
	BUILDING
①	MILEAGE
G	GATEWAY
S	STILE
FB	FOOTBRIDGE

THE SCALE OF THE
MAPS IS APPROXIMATELY
2½ INCHES PER MILE

NORTH IS ALWAYS AT THE TOP OF THE PAGE

LAND RANGER MAP 1:50000 REQUIRED FOR THE WALK
IS SHEET NO 194 DORCHESTER AND WEYMOUTH
(BRIDPORT IS JUST OFF THIS MAP BUT ONLY BY 2 MILES)

CHURCH OF St. PETER
AND St. PAUL

Take the A354 via Blandford Bridge. First right and a stile into the fields after 50 metres. Join a track and head for the woods. Pass the woods to the left. Crossing two fields and enter more woods. Go straight through the woods to a gate. Cross three fields to a road. Turn right then left onto a green road. Keep straight on through the woods.

QUARLESTON DOWN

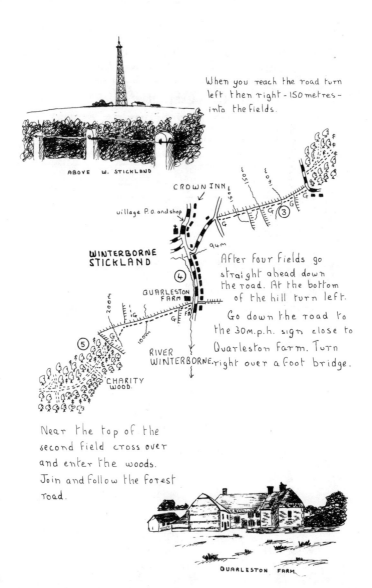

ABOVE W. STICKLAND

When you reach the road turn left then right - 150 metres - into the fields.

CROWN INN

village P.O. and shop

WINTERBORNE STICKLAND

QUARLESTON FARM

RIVER WINTERBORNE

CHARITY WOOD.

After four fields go straight ahead down the road. At the bottom of the hill turn left.

Go down the road to the 30m.p.h. sign close to Quarleston farm. Turn right over a foot bridge.

Near the top of the second field cross over and enter the woods. Join and follow the forest road.

QUARLESTON FARM

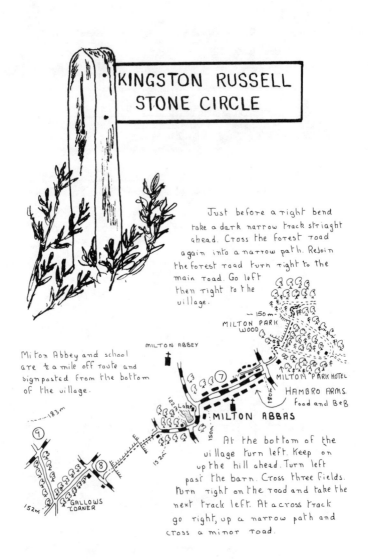

KINGSTON RUSSELL
STONE CIRCLE

Just before a right bend
take a dark narrow track straight
ahead. Cross the forest road
again into a narrow path. Rejoin
the forest road turn right to the
main road. Go left
then right to the
village.

~150 m~

MILTON PARK
WOOD

MILTON ABBEY

MILTON PARK HOTEL

HAMBRO ARMS
food and B&B

⑦

Milton Abbey and school
are ½ a mile off route and
signposted from the bottom
of the village.

MILTON ABBAS

183 m

⑨

⑧

152 m

152 m

150 m

GALLOWS
CORNER

At the bottom of the
village turn left. Keep on
up the hill ahead. Turn left
past the barn. Cross three fields.
Turn right on the road and take the
next track left. At a cross track
go right, up a narrow path and
cross a minor road.

22

THE FOX INN   LOWER ANSTEY.

■ THE FOX at LOWER ANSTEY.
food and accommodation. 3/4 mile off route,
closed all day Tuesday.

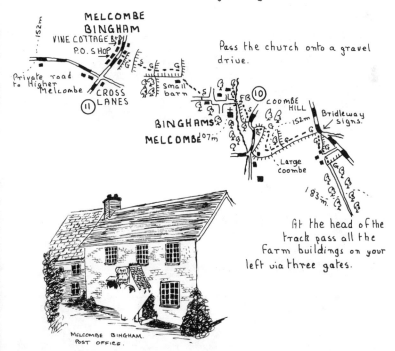

Pass the church onto a gravel drive.

At the head of the track pass all the farm buildings on your left via three gates.

MELCOMBE BINGHAM.
POST OFFICE.

DORSETSHIRE GAP

unfenced path through the woods

Go up the small path up the side of the earthwork.

BALL HILL

250m

overgrown path

FOLLY (farm track)

168m

14

250m

scrub hedge

13

12

183m

152m

HIGHER MELCOMBE

Before the buildings go into the fields. A sign points the way.

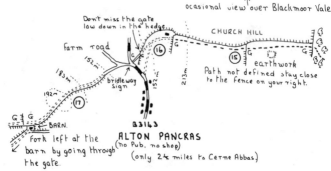

ocasional view over Blackmoor Vale

Don't miss the gate low down in the hedge.

CHURCH HILL

farm road

152m

16

183m

15

earthwork

192m

213m

17

152m

Path not defined stay close to the fence on your right.

bridleway sign

BARN

B3143

fork left at the barn by going through the gate.

ALTON PANCRAS
(no Pub, no shop)
(only 2½ miles to Cerne Abbas)

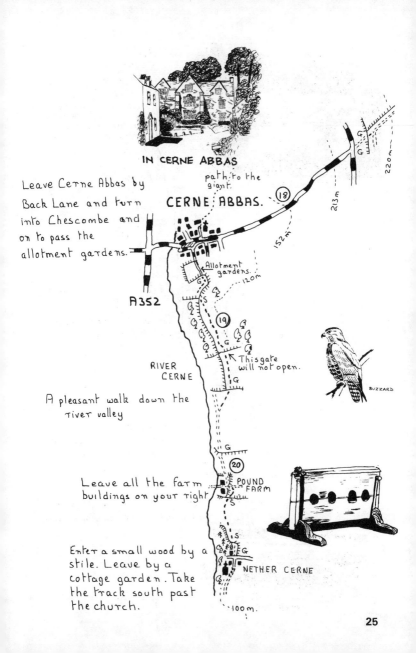

IN CERNE ABBAS

Leave Cerne Abbas by
Back Lane and turn
into Chescombe and
on to pass the
allotment gardens.

path to the giant.

CERNE ABBAS. ⑱

220 m
213 m
152 m

Allotment
gardens.
120 m

A352

⑲

RIVER
CERNE

This gate
will not open.

BUZZARD

A pleasant walk down the
river valley

⑳
POUND
FARM

Leave all the farm
buildings on your right

Enter a small wood by a
stile. Leave by a
cottage garden. Take
the track south past
the church.

NETHER CERNE

100 m.

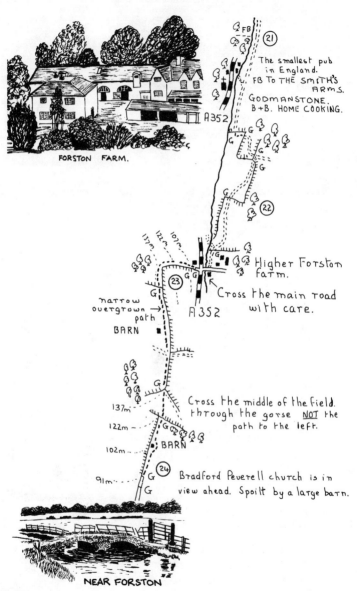

FORSTON FARM.

21

The smallest pub in England. FB TO THE SMITH'S ARMS. GODMANSTONE. B + B. HOME COOKING.

A352

22

Higher Forston farm.

Cross the main road with care.

23

narrow overgrown path

BARN

A352

Cross the middle of the field. through the gorse NOT the path to the left.

137m

122m

102m

BARN

91m

24

Bradford Peverell church is in view ahead. Spoilt by a large barn.

NEAR FORSTON

RAILWAY

RAILWAY AND A37

Turn left at the
main road.
...76 m

← STRATTON

A37

it is ¾ OF A MILE
to THE BULL INN. ←

RIVER FROME

BRADFORD
PEVERELL
NO PUB OR SHOP.

...76 m

25

Barns.

91m

FARM ROAD
......102 m

Turn left, down, to
follow the trees.
91m

26 ......91 m

FARM ROAD.

102 m

122 m

Dorchester
3 miles. →

THE LODGES

27

GREEN TRACK
G

122 m

107m

A35 Cross with
care the traffic
is fast here.

COTTAGE AT MARTINSTOWN

MARTINSTOWN

THE BREWERS ARMS
B3159

Turn right near the
church. There is a
bridleway sign near
a cottage.

Turn left at the
main road.
91m
P.O. SHOP.

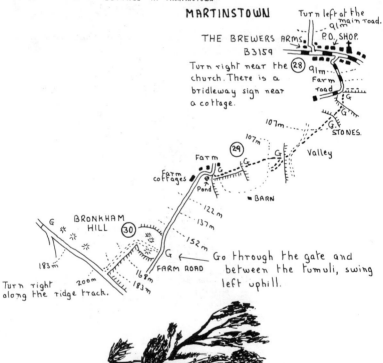

(28)

91m
Farm
road
G

107m

107m
G
G STONES.

(29)
G
G Valley

Farm
Farm
cottages
Pond
BARN

122m

137m

G
BRONKHAM
HILL
(30)

152m

183m
200m
168m
183m

G
FARM ROAD ← Go through the gate and
between the tumuli, swing
left uphill.

Turn right
along the ridge track.

PORTESHAM.

DANGER
LOW FLYING AIRCRAFT
KEEP TO
BRIDLE PATHS

Ignore the bridleway sign. You are going up the road to the Hardy Monument.

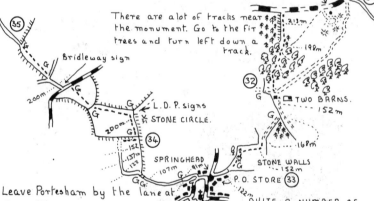

There are a lot of tracks near the monument. Go to the fir trees and turn left down a track.

(35)

Bridleway sign

200m

G

(31)

213m

198m

(32)

G   TWO BARNS.
152m

G

168m

G   L.D.P. signs
    STONE CIRCLE.

200m

G

(34)

152m

137m

122m

SPRINGHEAD

107m   91m

G

STONE WALLS
152m

P.O. STORE   (33)

Leave Portesham by the lane at Springhead and turn right onto a bridletrack.

Abbotsbury 2 miles

← B3157 →

PORTESHAM

76m

QUITE A NUMBER OF BED AND BREAKFAST PLACES, AND TWO PUBS.
THE KINGS ARMS. GOOD FOOD.

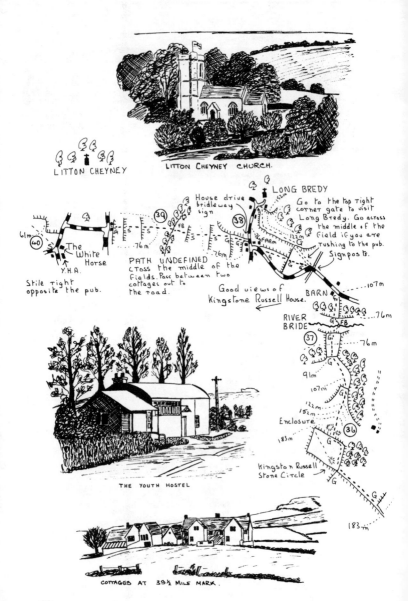

LITTON CHEYNEY

LITTON CHEYNEY CHURCH.

LONG BREDY

House drive
bridleway
sign

Go to the top right
corner gate to visit
Long Bredy. Go across
the middle of the
field if you are
rushing to the pub.
Signpost.

39

38

FARM

61m

40

The
White
Horse

Y.H.A.

Stile right
opposite the pub.

PATH UNDEFINED
Cross the middle of the
fields. Pass between two
cottages out to
the road.

76m

122m

Good views of
Kingstone Russell House.

BARN

107m

76m

RIVER
BRIDE

76m

37

91m

107m

122m

152m

Enclosure

183m

36

Kingston Russell
Stone Circle

183m

THE YOUTH HOSTEL

COTTAGES AT 39½ MILE MARK.

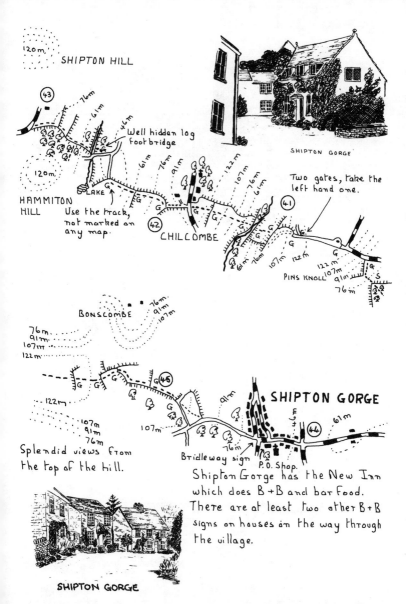

120m SHIPTON HILL

SHIPTON GORGE

43

76m
61m
46m Well hidden log
footbridge

120m

LAKE

HAMMITON HILL

Use the track, not marked on any map.

61m
76m
91m
122m
107m
76m
61m

Two gates, take the left hand one.

41

42

CHILCOMBE

107m 112m
122m
PINS KNOLL 107m
91m
76m

G S

BONSCOMBE
76m
91m
107m

76m
91m
107m
122m

122m

107m
91m
76m

Splendid views from the top of the hill.

G G 45

91m

SHIPTON GORGE

107m

76m

44

61m

Bridleway sign   P.O. Shop.

Shipton Gorge has the New Inn which does B + B and bar food. There are at least two other B + B signs on houses on the way through the village.

SHIPTON GORGE

BRIDPORT TOWN HALL.

The end of a splendid walk.
I was sorry to end this one.
When you come down from
the hill to a minor road
turn right then left at the
main road. Cross straight
over at the roundabout
   You will find the main street of
Bridport ahead. Shops cafes pubs.
The youth hostel is at the far end
of the town.

A3066

A35
Dorchester
14 miles.

47

BRIDPORT

To West Bay
1½ miles.

46

Lone
gate posts
122m
107m
91m
76m
61m
45m
30m
15m